
Bauhaus, Dessau

Phaidon Press Limited
Regent's Wharf
All Saints Street
London N1 9PA

Phaidon Press, Inc
180 Varick Street
New York, NY 10014

www.phaidon.com

First published 1993
This edition first published 2002
© 1993, 2002 Phaidon Press Limited
Photographs © 1993 Dennis Gilbert

ISBN 0 7148 4217 6

A CIP catalogue record for this book is available from the British Library

All rights reserved. No part of this publication may be reproduced, stored in a retrieval system or transmitted, in any form or by any means, electronic, mechanical, photocopying, recording or otherwise, without the written permission of Phaidon Press Limited.

Printed in Hong Kong

Acknowledgements: considerable help has been provided over recent years by working members of the Bauhaus in the preparation of parts of this text and I would like to thank Wolfgang Thöner, Bauhaus Research Fellow and Frau Louise Schier at Dessau for their interest in the project and for supplying archival material. Sincere thanks also go to Jasper Hermann for his help at the old Weimar Bauhaus and David Blake of Messrs Crittalls for information on steel window systems; to Nancy Jackson for her patient retyping of the many drafts of the text and to my wife, the architect Yasmin Shariff, for her critical advice and transference of the text into a more workable format. Illustrations were provided by: Hochschule für Architektur und Bauwesen, Weimar (4); Dennis Sharp (5, 7, 26); Bookart Architecture Picture Library (6, 24, 25, 39); Reinhard Friedrich* (15); Lucia Moholy* (34) and Walter Peterhaus* (37). *Bauhaus-Archiv, Berlin.

Bauhaus, Dessau
Walter Gropius

Dennis Sharp
ARCHITECTURE IN DETAIL

BAUHAUS

Walter Gropius on the Bauhaus, 1926

"The Bauhaus building, commissioned by the city of Dessau, was begun in autumn 1925, completed within one year and opened in December 1926.

The building covers a ground area of 113,400 sq ft and contains approximately 250,600 sq ft of floor space. It cost 902,500 marks, or 27.8 marks per cubic m of space, including all extra expenses. Purchase of the inventory amounted to 126,200 marks. The whole complex consists of three parts. The wing of the 'Technische Lehranstalten' (technical college, later called Berufsschule) contains administration and classrooms, staff room, library, physics laboratory, model rooms, fully finished basement, raised ground-floor and two upper floors. From the first and second floor a bridge on four columns spans the roadway.

The Bauhaus administration is on the first floor and the architectural department is on the second floor of it which leads to laboratories and classrooms of the Bauhaus. The stage workshop, printing shop, dye-works, sculpture studio, packing and stock rooms, caretaker's apartment and boiler room with a coal cellar extending in front of it, are in the basement. The carpentry shop and the exhibition rooms, large foyer and adjacent auditorium with raised stage extending in front of it, are on the raised ground floor. The weaving room, the rooms for basic instruction, a large lecture hall and the connection of building to building via the bridge, are on the first floor. The wall-painting shop, metalshop and two lecture halls, which can be combined into one large exhibition hall, are on the second floor. Adjacent is the second floor of the bridge with the rooms for the architectural department and the Gropius building office.

The auditorium on the elevated ground floor of this building leads to a one-storey, intermediate wing and to the studio building, which contains the recreational facilities for the students. The stage between auditorium and dining room can be opened at both ends for performances so that the spectators can sit on either side. On festive occasions, all stage walls can be opened, thus combining dining room, stage, auditorium and foyer into one large festival hall. The kitchen with its facilities is adjacent to the dining room. A spacious terrace overlooking a large sports field is in front of the dining room.

In the five upper floors of the studio building are twenty-eight studio apartments for students of the Bauhaus, with a kitchenette on each floor. The baths, gymnasium and changing rooms and an electric laundry are in the basement.

Material and construction of the entire complex: reinforced concrete skeleton and brick walls. Reinforced slabs on structural supports, in the basement 'mushroom supports'. Steel window sashes with double weathering contacts. The flat roofs on which one can walk, are covered with welded asphalt tiles on a tortoleum-insulated base; the flat roofs on which one cannot walk, with lacquered burlap over a tortoleum-insulated base covered with concrete. Drainage through cast iron pipes inside the buildings, dispensing with sheet zinc. Exterior finish of cement plaster painted with mineral paints.

The interior decoration of the entire building was done by the wall painting workshop of the Bauhaus. The design and execution of all light fixtures by the metal workshop of the Bauhaus. The tubular steel furniture in the auditorium, dining room and studios was made according to designs by Marcel Breuer. The lettering was executed by the print shop of the Bauhaus."

Walter Gropius, *Bauhaus*, issue 1, 1926, pp.2-3 (revised translation by Dennis Sharp).

'The Bauhaus was not an Institution... It was an idea', Mies van der Rohe, its last Director, said in Chicago in 1953. The institution lasted on three sites for fourteen years; the Bauhaus idea has proved indestructible.

The city of Dessau became the second official home of the Bauhaus in 1925 after 'Das Staatliche Bauhaus' had been forced to close for political reasons in Weimar. It had originally been founded in Weimar in 1919 out of the amalgamation of the existing Arts and Crafts school and the Weimar Academy of Fine Arts, with the architect Walter Gropius (1883–1969) as its Director, **1**. Dessau, the capital of Anhalt in central Germany was a progressive city with expanding industries – chemical, brown coal and aircraft manufacturing (Junkers) – within its region.

The simplified title 'Bauhaus' was transferred with the institution – after considerable negotiation – to Dessau where it became a city authority-financed college. It was designated a 'High School-for Design' and given university status. It was directly answerable to the Mayor and the City Council of Dessau.

When life at this enormously influential educational institution recommenced in Dessau the Bauhaus was more clearly dedicated to social ends and to the development of modern rational ideas for machine forms in art, design and architecture than in its Weimar years. The earlier Expressionistic, intuitive and rather confused German Romantic notions that had prevailed in Weimar no longer seemed relevant or applicable in the Bauhaus' new context. Times had changed. A key innovator in the Weimar school, Georg Muche later recorded that the changes he had seen at Dessau were fundamental and one of the major achievements of the Bauhaus' move. He also confessed that some of the earlier educational aims of the Bauhaus now appeared 'stupid and amateurish', not a term a German would use without considerable provocation. The economic conditions in Germany had also changed significantly in the Weimar Republic and the revaluation of the RMark in 1924 had led to new commercial expansion and confidence. The new Bauhaus built on such opportunities.

Bauhaus principles

The main principle of the 'unity between the arts' enunciated by Walter Gropius in his initial Weimar Bauhaus proclamation was still the guiding factor. It was largely adhered to at Dessau in order to underscore the newer ideas of mass production. Later, Gropius in his book *The New Architecture and The Bauhaus* (written in London in 1935) confirmed that the Bauhaus had been inaugurated with 'the specific object of realizing a modern architectonic art, which, like human nature, should be all-embracing in its scope. Within that sovereign federative union all the

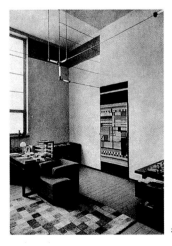

1 A portrait of Walter Gropius.
2 Lyonel Feininger's famous Bauhaus proclamation of 1919.
3 Gropius' office at Weimar was one of the first intimations of the new abstract geometrical style of the Dessau years.
4 The Bauhaus at Weimar utilized Van de Velde's original buildings. Today they form part of the Architectural Department of the University of Weimar.
5 The School of Applied Arts building, Weimar.
6 A portrait of Henri Van de Velde (1863–1957) taken at the time he ran the Weimar School of Applied Arts, a main component in Gropius' later Bauhaus.
7 Georg Muche's Haus am Horn at Weimar was the first real architectural experiment at the Bauhaus. It now serves as an archive of the Weimar Bauhaus.

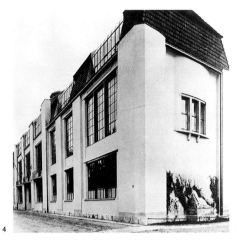

different "arts" … could be coordinated and find their appointed places'. It was a variation, of course, on the rather vague 19th century Wagnerian concept of the *Gesamtkunstwerk* or 'Total Work of Art'.[1] It was also an idea that had much in common with the ideas of the English Arts and Crafts movement that had been popularized by Hermann Muthesius. The symbolic idea of the Socialistic *Zukunftskathedrale* ('Future Cathedral') depicted by Lyonel Feininger in his famous Bauhaus proclamation cover, **2**, however, proved like a red rag to the bullish conservatives of Weimar who eventually forced the Bauhaus out of their city.

Weimar to Dessau – an uncomfortable transition
The move to Dessau from the old German city proved challenging and traumatic. It was forced on Gropius by growing political resentment in the city towards the Bauhaus and its increasingly international and 'foreign' character, **3**. The trouble came to a head in August 1923, the time of the Bauhaus' first Open Exhibition and Lecture Week. Johannes Itten had left in Easter to be replaced by the Hungarian Constructivist László Moholy-Nagy as Director of the Preliminary Course. Josef Albers, a recently graduated Bauhaus student, took up a position as his assistant. The aim of the Bauhaus week was to appeal to the world to save the institution from closure, **4**, **5**.[2]

Bauhaus week attracted an enormous number of visitors. Some estimates suggest 15,000. Although the exhibition itself and the week of special events that accompanied it were a tremendous national and international success it breached rather than healed the differences that had been developing for some time between the Bauhaus and the Weimar city authorities. The city authorities had demanded that the public should see what was going on in the Bauhaus and the exhibition, which used both Van de Velde buildings, was certainly seen as a direct initiative meeting this request, **6**. The citizens of Weimar did not like what they saw.

One of the main features of the Bauhaus Exhibition was the Haus am Horn (The House on the Horn) designed by the painter Georg Muche, **7**. A white cubic 'functional' single-storey atrium-type house unit, it was ostensibly meant to be a prototypical unit for a larger estate of houses. Now used as an unofficial archive of the Bauhaus' Weimar period it can be seen as one of the first building blocks in the new architecture of the time. It was part of a development of an earlier design by Walter Gropius for a whole estate of houses which had not proved acceptable to the student body.

Muche's model house was constructed on the edge of Weimar's famous city park in a prestigious wooded area. Unlike the craft-based timber-clad Sommerfeld Villa of

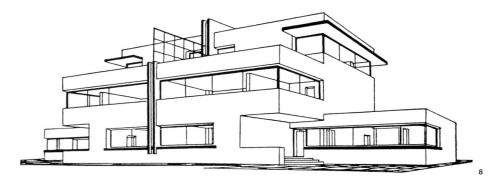

1920 – which had been the Bauhaus' other practical student-based product – the Haus am Horn was an early example of prefabrication with elements constructed and assembled on site (cf. Gropius' later Törten Estate house units in Dessau). Muche's project was financed by Adolf Sommerfeld, the Berlin-based contractor and timber merchant whose patronage often extended to Bauhaus experiments and designs.[3]

During the period of the exhibition Walter Gropius presented his lecture on 'Art and Technology: A New Unity' which looked forward to a progressive attitude in German industry as it moved from its craft-oriented base to the new methods of modern machine-based mass production. It was a significant contribution to the new rational thinking of the time.

Political unrest
As a new national government was elected in Berlin further unrest grew throughout the whole country and Gropius himself, known for his left wing attitudes, was investigated by the military authorities. Nothing was pinned on him. However, the Nazis gradually took over the regional government of Anhalt and the Bauhaus (which was always seen as an organization harbouring suspect figures) was soon under investigation. It was accused of neglecting German cultural values and encouraging Jewish influence amongst its teachers and students. Furthermore, there were Bolsheviks too, under the Bauhaus beds in the form of foreign 'Masters', Kandinsky and Moholy-Nagy. Objective scrutiny soon turned into vengeful action and eventually the Bauhaus' grant was cut in half.

Simultaneously the Bauhaus staff were given suspended dismissal notices. In March 1925 it was announced that the Weimar State Bauhaus was to close. Several liberal and progressive German cities offered to take in the institution.

The offer made by the socialist democratic city of Dessau – conveniently placed mid-way between Weimar and Berlin – through the generous initiative of the city's progressive Mayor Dr Fritz Hesse (with Ludwig Grote, Director of the Dessau Art Museum) proved the most acceptable to Gropius and the 'Masters' of the Weimar school. It was agreed to move lock, stock and barrel to Dessau. This acceptance acknowledged that much greater opportunities resided in a city like Dessau with its radical political base. It was also the site of the Junkers aircraft factory, a fact that did not escape the notice of the RAF during the Second World War.

The move was also to provide Gropius with a wider role. He was to become responsible for the running and organization of the city's *Kunstgewerbeschule* and Trade School, neither of which were to be amalgamated with the Bauhaus. Fortunately, the Mayor also believed in the Bauhaus principles and envisaged that it would aid the extension of a new kind of education related to modern ideas in the city.

It was to Gropius' great advantage that there was no building to go to. He was thus able to tailor-make a new 'Bauhaus' on the Friedrichsalle, some 2km from the city centre. Meanwhile, he opened his new architectural practice in the centre of Dessau, although without his partner Adolf Meyer with whom he had worked so closely during his early years. Meyer had opted to remain behind in Weimar. Gropius was unable to persuade the authorities in Dessau to fund a separate architecture department in the new Bauhaus so he again employed students as apprentices and assistants in his private office as he had done in Weimar. It is estimated that as many as twenty-four members of staff worked in the practice in Dessau, during the three years from 1925–28.

The Bauhaus building process
Design work on the new main building began almost immediately Gropius arrived in Dessau. It was soon approved in principle by the city authorities. The complex that emerged emphasized, in both functional and symbolic terms, Gropius' revised educational and architectural programmes. Clearly there were no longer to be any

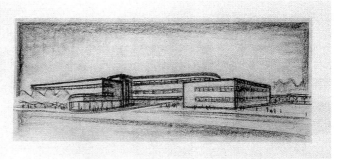

8 In 1923 Carl Fieger prepared a design for semi-detached houses for dentists in Dessau.
9, 10 Carl Fieger's preliminary sketches for the Dessau Bauhaus building, 1925.
11 Fieger's sketch showing the incorporation of a number of major changes, including the student *Prellerhaus*.
12 An aerial view of the Bauhaus taken at the time of construction.

compromises in these aims. By the middle of the summer of 1925 the drawings were complete. Work commenced on the green field site in September of that year and the new Bauhaus was inaugurated a couple of months later than had originally been planned, on 4 December 1926. Sigfried Giedion had referred to it as 'Gropius' greatest achievement'.[4] In the 1960s, Reyner Banham was to give it the status of a 'sacred site'. 'More than a manifesto, it was a masterpiece.'[5]

Scheme design

The scheme design went through a number of changes as it emerged on the drawing board. At the same time the office was also involved in the creation of three semi-detached houses for the main teachers of the Bauhaus: Klee, Kandinsky, Moholy-Nagy, Schlemmer, Schmidt and Fieger, as well as a detached house for Gropius himself. With the exception of the Director's own house (which was later destroyed in a bombing raid) the other 'double' houses remain intact today, although in need of renovation.

The cost of the new building was met directly by grants from the city of Dessau. The amount earmarked for new construction and upkeep was in the region of RMark 1 m. However, the time gap in the construction process meant that the new buildings would not be ready for a some time.

The 'Institute of Design', as the Bauhaus was now designated, was established in temporary factory and warehouse accommodation. Also, some of the 'Masters' were still living in Weimar and had to travel to Dessau to teach each week. The students – many of them almost poverty stricken – found accommodation in various parts of the town and only attended studio teaching in a sporadic way, rather like the students at the Architectural Association in London after the mid-1930s when it began to model its design studios on those of the Bauhaus.

The running of the Gropius office was now in the hands of the 25-year-old and thoroughly efficient Ernst Neufert, a former Bauhaus architecture student (1919–20) whom Gropius had employed in his Weimar atelier. Neufert was so efficient, Reginald Isaacs claims in his biography *Walter Gropius: An Illustrated Biography of the Creator of the Bauhaus*, that he was responsible for throwing out all of Gropius' early drawings and sketches, a man 'whose sense of history was subordinate to his sense of efficiency'.[6] As well as his position as the office manager for the Bauhaus jobs he also taught architecture classes at the Bauhaus. Later he was appointed head of architecture at the Bauhochschule in Weimar – Gropius' old school!

Carl Fieger, it appears, was largely responsible for making a series of preliminary sketches in 1925 that began to give a true idea of what Walter Gropius had in mind for the new Bauhaus buildings. These drawings gave an impression of what would eventually be built on the suburban site to the south of Dessau city centre.

Fieger's early perspective drawings showed three main elements: a spacious four-storey workshop wing featuring a fully-glazed facade with pronounced mullions, a separate school wing, and a raised joint administration block which linked these two components above a roadway, **9–11**. This rather futuristic bridge spanning the roadway, the Bauhausstrasse, led to an estate area (not developed until much later) and helped to define architecturally the two main functional units of the Arts and Crafts school and the Bauhaus. A Fieger planning scheme of a year or so later linked this new road with the network that connects the Bauhaus, a sports stadium arena and the railway station.[7]

By most institutional standards the Bauhaus itself was tiny, **12**. Its size, however, belied the enormous symbolic significance it was to gain as its national and international reputation grew as an experimental and commercial laboratory for design and after 1927 (when the architecture department got underway) as a hotbed of architecture and (somewhat later) urban design. Today it is being considered as the pivotal element in the creation of a 'Future Bauhaus' proposal by the German state of Sachsen-Anhalt to house the architecture, building, engineering and design facilities of a new

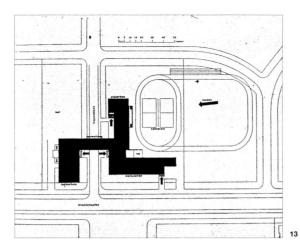

13

technical university sited between the Bauhaus site and city centre.

Basic designs

Disappointingly there is little evidence available on the development of the basic architectural design ideas that lie behind the Bauhaus building itself. Nor is there much circumstantial evidence. All the drawings it appears were destroyed. Even Gropius' own otherwise definitive study of the built buildings, *Bauhausbauten Dessau* (1930), the 12th volume in the famous *Bauhausbucher* series, which he edited with Moholy-Nagy, gives little indication of the actual design process or the details of the construction. Giedion in his definitive *Walter Gropius Team and Teamwork* (1954), only provides an appraisal in summary. Furthermore, both books fail to indicate the progress of the concept through its sketch and design development stages. From more recently acquired evidence it appears that much of the preliminary design work was carried out by the students of the Bauhaus course under Carl Fieger, his chief draftsperson and detailer.[8]

Carl Fieger was born in 1893 in Mainz, the city in which he later trained as an architect before commencing work in Peter Behrens' office in Berlin, prior to joining Gropius in Weimar. Gropius worked in Behrens' office in 1907 (at the same time as Mies and Le Corbusier) where he also met his partner Adolf Meyer. Fieger went to Gropius' office in Dessau where he also acted as an architectural teacher at the Bauhaus. Interestingly he had produced a project for a pair of semi-detached houses for a site in Dessau in 1923, **8**. Recent speculation seems to support the view that Fieger was responsible with Gropius for developing the Bauhaus building's basic form and layout. The perspective drawings reinforce this view. The first, a hesitant, probative sketch indicates a complex of loosely connected buildings spread out, spatially, on the site. Service functions were to one side with access for the supply of coal to the bunkers and to the sports field. Asymmetrically placed (and it seems not to have been deviated from in any of the later designs) were the twin entrances. They faced each other across the well-defined roadway, the bridge over which clearly differentiated their separate functions. On the Bauhaus side a 'form of living' with educational, work, social and living functions grouped together, was also achieved, **13, 14**.

The brief for the new building was thus achieved by adopting a functional layout and a whole series of new disciplines. These provided it with an economical and efficient 'modern school' basis in which the title 'Master' (derived from the medieval guilds) was replaced by Professor, and the terms 'journeyman' and 'apprentice' were neatly reduced to 'student'. Lessons were renamed 'lectures' to confirm the new image of a technical college. Workshops with one director (an artist) and one instructor (a craftsman) were superseded.

A five-storey studio block with twenty-eight student bedrooms was later added to Fieger's next design and an auditorium and canteen were shown located on the first floor. This was to become the hub of the whole enterprise, an area that could be opened up in order to create a large interconnected, communal, performance and exhibition space. Work, living, eating, parties and theatrical performance were thus united in what has been called the 'miniature world of the Bauhaus'.[9]

Bauhaus interiors: colour, planes and chairs

Considerable interest was shown in the use of colour in buildings in the Bauhaus workshop courses both at Weimar and Dessau. This is perfectly understandable as much emphasis was placed in both places on the work of painters and on colour theory in the Bauhaus. This work was taken into the realm of architecture, or at least interior design, by Herbert Bayer at Weimar with his murals for the secondary staircases during the 1923 Exhibition and in the project for the Director's new office. These staircase murals have recently been fully restored.

In 1926, during the time of the construction, Hinnerk Scheper produced proposals for the exterior colouring of

14

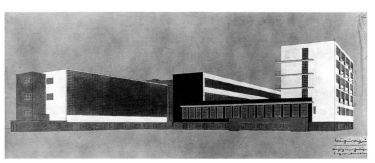

15

13 Site plan of the Bauhaus in Dessau.
14 The Bauhaus building under construction.
15 The proposed colour scheme plan was prepared by Hinnerk Scheper who was also responsible for the interior colours. In the event, the interior scheme was not used; external colours were restricted to white, black and grey.
16 Furniture and fittings were designed by Marcel Breuer and his students. Reconstructions of the contemporary light fittings were made when the building was renovated in 1976.
17 A contemporary caricature of Walter Gropius by B.F. Dolbin published in the *Magdeburger Zeitung* on 16 October 1927.
18 A contemporary cartoon by H.M. Lindhoff captioned 'Above the ruins of the house you can hear Mr Gropius moan', published in *Kladderadatsch* on 4 March 1928.

17

the main Dessau Bauhaus facades, **15**.¹⁰ The proposed colours were dark and light grey and brown with a predominantly white finish reserved for the rendered faces of the workshop, college, administrative and student blocks. Doors were to be highlighted in process red. Most of the furniture and fittings for the new Bauhaus were designed by the newly appointed 'Professor' Marcel Breuer and his joinery workshop students. He prepared designs for use in the studios, theatre auditorium and canteen, **16**. Here, tubular steel furniture was used for the first time on a large scale. In the theatre itself he introduced chairs with steel tubular supports and seating and armrests made from hard-wearing, taut hessian.

The lamp fittings used in the buildings were produced by the metal workshop, most of them designed by Max Kraals and Marianne Brandt.

The signs in the building were carried out by members of the print workshop while the mural painting class was responsible for decorating many of the rooms. A contemporary report records the effect: 'the individual classrooms – and above all the library – are gently shaded in light tones. Beams are logically highlighted in specific colours. The School's dinning room works particularly well and the tripartite ceiling is picked out in red and black whilst, where there are no windows, the walls remain entirely white'.¹¹

At Dessau, with all this design activity and economic self-help, it could be demonstrated that the arts and crafts had been brought together in a unified whole which emphasized the collaborative nature of the many arts connected with building.

Contemporary reactions to the appearance of the new Bauhaus were mixed, **17**, **18**. On the one hand conservative critics could slam into Gropius for his persistent use of flat roofs which Schulze-Naumburg found 'inappropriate to the German climate and customs'. While another critic, Konrad Nonn, Editor of *Zentralblatt der Bauverwaltung*, tried to prove that Gropius' use of flat roofs and glass walls were 'wholly impractical' and not 'founded on *Handwerk* as Gropius claims'. He went on: 'in the Bauhaus buildings... functional purpose is suppressed in the name of a fad in taste, and the result is the opposite of what we (i.e. *Zentralblatt der Bauverwaltung*) usually call "modern functionalism"'.¹²

Contemporary Modernist critics on the other hand, from Müller-Wulckow to Behne and the Russian writer Ilya Ehrenburg, were ecstatic. Perhaps Ehrenburg's graphic eye-witness accounts will suffice to establish the buildings' credentials:

'I approached the Bauhaus on one of the first days of spring. Delicate mists rose from the thicket of industrial chimneys; in the skies Junkers planes buzzed merrily

18

16

19 A contemporary photograph of the famous Bauhaus workshop facade.
20 An aerial view of the Bauhaus showing the development of the surroundings.
21 The glass wall played an important role in Gropius' early architecture as this section through the staircase at the Werkbund Exhibition model factory of 1914 shows.
22 As late as 1924 Gropius was still designing in the Wrightian manner. Study for the school pavilion for the Fröbel organization at Bad Liebenstein in Thuringia.
23 Perspective of Gropius' factory and offices for Kappe and Co., Alfeld-an-der-Leine, 1924.
24 Study for the design of the International Academy by Gropius in Erlangen, 1924.
25 The industrial city of Kharkov which Reyner Banham compared with the Dessau Bauhaus.

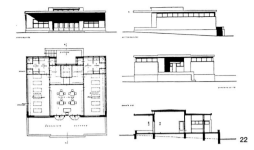
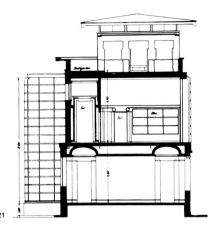

about, and there was a smell of March in the air and of smoke and chalk. When I finally saw the Bauhaus which seems to be cast of one piece like a persistent thought, and its glass walls which form a transparent angle, united with the air and yet separated from it by a distinct will – I stopped instinctively. It wasn't surprise in the face of a sensible invention, no – it was simply admiration'.[13]

There are numerous other epistles of ecstasy recorded on seeing the manifestations of a new architecture in Dessau in 1926, **19**.[14]

There really was no other building in Europe quite like Gropius' Bauhaus, **20**. It was, Banham has written, 'the first unmistakable harbinger of an international style'.[15] The stuttering Wright derived that Modernism, seen in Gropius' pre-war factories at Alfeld-an-der-Leine and at Cologne was replaced by an articulate and somewhat complex language of simple cubic forms, transparent surfaces and elegant internal spaces, **21**. The transitional period, when Gropius and Adolf Meyer were practicing, saw a deliberate change towards the simplification of the architectural object. Nothing in contemporary German architecture would ever be the same again. Followed by the international demonstration of Modernist tendencies a year later in Stuttgart on the Weissenhof the Bauhaus has a special place in the development of modern architectural principles. Having moved away from Wrightian precepts, **22** (borrowed from the pages of the famous Wasmuth publications) and a short Expressionist phrase, Gropius moved with his partner (and former colleague from the Behrens office) Adolf Meyer, towards the rationalistic *Sachlichkeit*. In schemes such as the *Chicago Tribune* Tower competition entry, the Kappe Factory, Alfeld-an-der-Leine, **23**, the Auerbach House at Jena and principally the International Philosophical Academy for Erlangen (1924), **24**, an anticipation or foreshadowing of the Bauhaus buildings' main characteristics can be observed. Gropius' design reflected above all the mood of the times towards internationalism, as well as to the reduction of formal elements in design. Like De Stijl painting, in a sense, the Bauhaus was composed of basically related functional elements that produced a cohesive interrelated asymmetrical whole. As Banham wrote in his *Theory and Design in the First Machine Age*, 'The planning is ... like nothing else of the period in its centrifugal organization ... Equally new and rare is the mode of vision – the emphasis in (the book) *Bauhausbauten Dessau* is the first and foremost on a set of air views of the buildings ... The three-dimensional quality of the planning is also remarkable, with two storeys of the school bridged across the road...' and here Banham compares the Russian Constructivist work at Kharkov, **25**.[16]

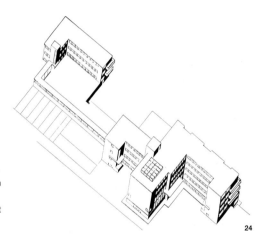

Ehrenburg felt the Bauhaus said something about 'the triumph of clarity'. He wrote, 'for the first time the earth sees here a cult of naked reason... every angle, every line, each of the smallest details repeats insistently the closing words of theorems, forgotten since schooldays: "what was to be proven"'.[17]

Compositional elements: corporeality
With the new Bauhaus building Gropius underlined the notion of the building as a 'total work' of compositional architecture. It was a clear articulation of built form that possessed none of the simple-minded functionalism of other contemporary modern structures. Early as it was, it appeared as a mature example of the *neues Bauen* which was no longer dependent on the Wrightian references that had been associated with Gropius' earlier pre-war work. In its report of the opening of the Bauhaus in Dessau, a 1926 issue of *Kunst and Künstler* underlined this architectural maturity:

'The new buildings for the Academy and workshops can indeed be recognized as a model of today's architectural achievements. The consistent exploitation of the potential of the new materials and methods has enabled the problems posed by a major project to be solved in exemplary fashion. The plan of the building, which consists of three individual but intimately connected parts has been most carefully thought out, and functional requirements are met within a whole which, in the disposition of space alone, creates an impressive effect'.[18]

Describing this intimate connection and the layout of the buildings' compositional elements, Walter Gropius compared the complexities of its design to aspects of historical architecture. 'The typical building of the Renaissance or the Baroque has a symmetrical facade, an approach leading up to its central axis... .' He claimed, furthermore, that it eschewed classical models. 'A building produced in the spirit of our times rejects the imposing model of the symmetrical facade. You have to walk right round the whole building in order to appreciate its corporeality and the function of its various parts'[19], **26**.

Besides the functional and windmill-shaped plan, what caught most commentators' imagination was the appearance of the outside of the workshop building as a see-through glazed block, **27**. Transparency was no longer simply an illusion – it could be seen here as a practical effect. It gave the building a dramatic quality creating an effect that Arthur Korn later said gave the feeling that it was '*Da und nicht Da*' – 'there and yet not there'.

The huge curtain window wrapped itself around the corner and receded back to the main Bauhaus entrance. It emphasized the 'mechanical' and the open spatial nature of the new architecture. Internally, the workshop spaces were flooded with light. Inevitably this caused internal over-heating on sunny days. At night the exterior lit up like an illuminated box providing a mature example of the new German '*Lichtarchitektur*'. There was as much window as wall on the workshop facade of this building. The load-bearing columns were (as Le Corbusier demanded) recessed back from the main walls and the whole of the workshop building could be viewed as a huge expanse of industrial glass windows. This, the predominant element in the design, was carefully linked in one direction by a two-storey administrative bridge. The student studio/bedroom accommodation of the *Prellerhaus*[20] which lay on the far side of the site overlooked portly villas and the wooded areas of Dessau.

The composition of Gropius' building could be appreciated at the time as a complete object in the landscape rather than as it is today, as part of an expanded city. The compositional idea was simply expressed. The main road frontage with its simple flat roofs was a three-storey horizontal shape poised over a recessed but half-exposed basement. Its horizontality was in direct contrast to the single vertical feature, the rear student block. On the south corner of the workshop block large letters, BAUHAUS, explained the new building's purpose.

26 'You have to walk right round the whole building in order to appreciate its corporeality and the function of its various parts' wrote Walter Gropius. This sequence of photographs goes around the Bauhaus in an anti-clockwise fashion.

27 A view looking from the administrative wing towards the workshop block.

28 The 'free-standing' glazed workshop wall with the line of radiators behind.
29, 30 Many types of opening lights were introduced from the Fenestra-Crittall range, from the hopper to the mechanically-operated 'range' of windows.
31 A night-time shot looking across the administrative bridge facade.

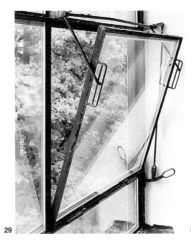

Bauhaus construction
The construction of the building was conventionally modern with an in-situ reinforced-concrete skeletal framework, with the columns exposed on the inside of the building, **28**. The infill brick walls were rendered on the outside to receive the white painted finish. Reinforced hollow clay tile floors were supported on beams running between the columns. At basement level a sturdier structural concrete mushroom column head was introduced. The flat roofs were covered with a new proprietary roofing material (which failed disastrously some years later) while the roof to the student block was covered with concrete slabs and designed as an external roof terrace. Universal section steel windows were used throughout with double-weather contacts and plate glass, **29, 30**. These were similar in pattern to the windows used earlier in Alfeld-an-der-Leine's *Faguswerke* administrative block.

Functional layout
The workshop block at basement level contained the stage, printing and sculpture workshops as well as ancillary rooms for dyeing and storage. It also housed the heating services and the boilers which were fuelled by local brown coal. The ground-floor plan provided for a joinery workshop with large display rooms before it

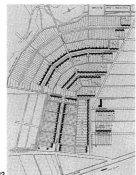

merged into the studio wing with its auditorium. The weaving workshops and preliminary course classrooms were situated on the second floor while the administrative offices extended on the lower floor of the bridge that led to the technical school. Situated on the second floor were the metalwork and wall painting workshops. This level also incorporated the two expandable lecture rooms adjacent to the upper floor of the bridge in which Gropius' architectural practice was housed. Later the architecture department, under the Swiss, Hannes Meyer, occupied this whole bridge wing, **31**. The so-called 'Technical School' wing contained most of the other administrative offices and staff rooms as well as the model-making workshops and library.

The key social elements in the whole design were the theatre auditorium and the canteen which were situated in the single-storey section that connected the workshop block with the student wing. The kitchens that supplied the canteen were located on the ground floor of the student block under which were the gymnasium plus additional storage space.

The five-storey studio block itself contained twenty-eight apartments and provided students with a shared kitchen on each floor. Sixteen of the apartments had projecting balconies facing east which were popular points for student *poseurs* and artists who performed when parties and festivities took place in the buildings or when home-movies were being made.

Bauhaus revival

In 1976, at the time of the 50th anniversary of its opening, the Bauhaus was fully restored by the German Democratic Republic, **37**. The conservation office of the Dessau City Architect's Department was responsible for the work itself. A considerable amount of finance and conservation expertise was put into the restoration and this has proved sufficient to enable it to withstand the vagaries of the local climate and use over the past seventeen years. More recently, additional renovation work has been carried out and on the whole it is still in remarkably good condition. However, the steel workshop windows originally manufactured by Fenestra-Crittall with their universal steel sections, were carefully replaced by new extruded section aluminium ones. These remain in good working order. The canteen still operates successfully for staff, students and visitors and the famous cubic-shaped auditorium has been carefully re-furnished with copies of the Breuer steel and hessian-linked chairs, **38**, **39**.

Professorial houses

Having suffered from decades of neglect the professors' houses are still in a distressed condition, **33**, **34**. A year or so ago rendered surfaces had spalled and render had peeled away; the original plain brickwork was exposed in places; broken windows and the unkempt landscaped surroundings showed the extent of years of neglect. The villa designed for and occupied by Gropius and his wife had also formed part of this group of houses before it was bombed during the war. Now only the basement and part of the garage remain. The original house has been replaced by a squarish pitched-roofed bungalow.

The six units on the site (the three *Döppelhauser*) are important examples of the architectural language of the mid-1920s with their new cubic, clear-cut functional forms. Their construction had begun in the summer of 1925 and like the Bauhaus they were rendered and had troublesome flat roofs. Each was designed by Gropius as a generous spacious, individual unit incorporating internal studios, living and bedroom accommodation. Most of them had external roof terraces. It is said that Gropius never refused to carry out any of the numerous last minute alterations demanded by the professors' wives.

Gropius' success at Dessau was confirmed by a number of commissions by the city authorities. Some buildings in the Dessau area not related directly to the Bauhaus were designed in Gropius' architectural office, for example the Labour Exchange in the city centre, **36**; a highly original single-storey top-lit building with semi-

32 Prefabricated housing units with an original, unaltered façade on the left.
33, 34 The Masters' houses in a nearby wooded area in Dessau, still in urgent need of renovation.
35 General plan of the Törten Estate, Dessau, 1926–30.
36 Walter Gropius' Labour Exchange, Dessau, 1929.
37 The original studio layout in the architecture section.
38, 39 The workshop block has many uses today, laid out (left) as studio space and (right) as an exhibition hall.

40

circular plan, and the first stage of an experimental estate of workers' standard house units which grew in three phases from 1926–30, **32**, **35**.

The cooperative store and flats of the *Konsumverein* of 1928 – one of Gropius' last Dessau designs – provided the central feature for the Törten Estate, **40**. Today, it still plays an important role on the estate as a shop, community centre and café, but like its surrounding houses is also in urgent need of refurbishment. All the single-house units on the estate have been altered and extended bar one which is a token symbol to Gropius' original interiors.

One of the more controversial buildings erected in Dessau Törten was an experimental 'steel house' designed by the Bauhaus weaving workshop Master, Georg Muche, in conjunction with Richard Paulick (who was later to run Gropius' architectural office in Berlin), **41**. It contributed – as a practical exemplar – to the lively discussions on standardization going on at the time in the Bauhaus itself with Hannes Meyer and others. Gropius was not at all happy with the design although a year later at Stuttgart he developed a similar prefabricated structure on the Weissenhof. Restored in 1976 it is undergoing refurbishment again and will soon be closely linked to the Bauhaus. The original design was based on the use of prefabricated steel sheet metal panels and column supports. It was site-assembled on a concrete foundation.

Muche's steel house had a history. He recalled in the *Bauhaus Journal* (1927) that its design ideas went back to the time he was experimenting with the Haus am Horn erected at the Weimar Bauhaus Exhibition in 1923. It was designed as a single-storey, flexible and extensible family unit. But, at the time Muche confessed, 'all types of steel constructions for houses are still primitive'. Also it needed far too much steel, a point that was rectified by Gropius' more economical housing in Stuttgart in 1927.

Near the steel house, and on the same edge of the Törten Estate, Carl Fieger designed his own very individualistic family house in 1927, **42**. The two-storey rendered house, which has suffered from neglect and an unsympathetic extension, incorporated a fine curved staircase tower that led up to a narrow bedroom wing forming one side of the L-shaped design. The re-entrant thus formed was filled by the living room. The roof of this living room served as a sun terrace to the bedrooms.

One of the most reassuring aspects of the revival of the Bauhaus is that it symbolizes the strength and purposes of Modern architecture, art and design. The Dessau Bauhaus and its predecessor at Weimar are today seeking a new identity which, once the traumatic conditions of reunification are resolved and new aims established, will again focus attention on the original venues. In *Idee und Aufbau* Gropius wrote about the way he saw the Bauhaus:

'Its responsibility is to educate men and women to understand the world they live in and to invent and create forms symbolizing that world'.[21] That was 1923. In 1935 whilst in London he enlarged on his ideas: 'Our ambition was to arouse the creative artist from his other worldliness and reintegrate him into the workaday world of realities: and at the same time to broaden and humanize the rigid almost exclusive material mind of the businessman. Thus our informing conception of the basic unity of all design in relation to life was in diametrical opposition to that of "art for art's sake" and to the even more dangerous philosophy it sprang from: business as an end in itself'.[22]

The pertinency of such views is clearly still with us. They reflect a current problem as architecture emerges out of a difficult and by all accounts posthumous phase of anti-Modernism. Who would now believe there is any relevance for example in Tom Wolfe's contention that Gropius' aim was after all only a loony battle over the lost bourgeoisie.[23] As we move today into the arena of 'Design Build' in which the new business managers (unnumbered and mainly untrained and unfailingly incompetent and unschooled in matters architectural) take over the role of designer in order to fit a preordained budget in a undeveloped design, it becomes obvious that a unique experiment like that of Gropius' Bauhaus has much more than passing historical significance.

41

42

40 The *Konsumverein*, a seven-storey apartment block and community information centre.
41 George Muche's steel house at Dessau Törten was renovated in 1976 but has since been neglected as this picture taken in 1990 indicates.
42 Carl Fieger's own house, Dessau Törten.

Notes
1 Walter Gropius, *The New Architecture and the Bauhaus*, London, 1935. Trans. P. Morton Shand.
2 See S. Giedion, 'Bauhaus, v Bauhaus woche zu Weimar', *Das Werk*, Vol X, 1923.
3 See G. Muche, *Ein Versuchshaus des Bauhaus*, Weimar, 1923.
4 S. Giedion, *Walter Gropius*, London, 1954, p.43.
5 R. Banham, *Guide to Modern Architecture*, London, 1962, p.148.
6 R. Isaacs, *Walter Gropius*, Boston, 1991, p.126.
7 See plan in C. Engelmann and C. Shädlich, *Die Bauhausbauten in Dessau*, Berlin, 1991, p.21.
8 See for example, Isaacs, op. cit., pp.72 and 151 and Engelmann and Shädlich, op. cit. The latter shows the development of Fieger's sketch schemes.
9 A vivid account of life in the Bauhaus at Dessau is given by T. Lux Feininger in *Bauhaus and Bauhaus People*, New York, 1970, pp.173–94.
10 For a review of Scheper's colour work see H. Dearstyne and D. Spaeth (ed.), *Inside the Bauhaus*, London, 1986, pp.148–9.
11 See M. Droste, *Bauhaus 1919–33*, Berlin, 1990, p.123.
12 B. Miller Lane, *Architecture and Politics in Germany 1918–45*, Cambridge, Mass., 1968, pp.134–5.
13 From an article in the *Frankfurter Zeitung*, 1926.
14 However, the penetration of those ideas in England was slow and faltering. Although not initially affected by the growing premonition of war that obscured later German developments in the arts from the British gaze after 1932 nothing will be found on the Dessau Bauhaus, for example, in the annals of the AA or RIBA until well into the 1930s.
15 Banham, op. cit., p.287.
16 Banham, op. cit., p.287.
17 From an article in the *Frankfurter Zeitung*, 1926.
18 Quoted in S. Giedion, *Space, Time and Architecture*, 4th edn, London, 1941.
19 Gropius *idem*, p.58.
20 Named after the earlier student atelier at Weimar.
21 From W. Gropius, *The Scope of Total Architecture*, London, 1956, p.23.
22 Gropius, op. cit., p.24.
23 Tom Wolfe, *From Bauhaus to Our House*, London, 1982, pp.10–13.

Chronology
March 1919 Opening of 'Das Staatliche Bauhaus' in Weimar
September 1925 Bauhaus closes in Weimar Commission for the new Bauhaus to be combined with the Dessau Technical College
4 December 1926 Bauhaus opens in Dessau
1926 Masters' houses constructed
1 October 1932 Dessau Bauhaus closes and staff and students moved to Berlin-Steglitz. It was later taken over as a Nazi training school
11 April 1933 The Bauhaus in Berlin is finally closed by the Nazis
1976 The Bauhaus is refurbished by the German Democratic Republic and reopened as 'The Bauhaus, Dessau'

Bibliography
Comprehensive bibliographies on Walter Gropius and the Bauhaus can be found in a number of major primary sources including:

The American Association of Architectural Bibliographers, *Walter Gropius: A Bibliography Part 1*, Vol 1, 1965, pp.23–43. This was followed by Vol 111, *Walter Gropius*, 1966.
Sharp, Dennis, *Sources of Modern Architecture, A Critical Bibliography: Walter Gropius*, London, 1981, pp.53–4.
Wingler, H.M., *The Bauhaus: Weimar Dessau Berlin Chicago*, Cambridge, Mass., 1969, pp.627–47.

Publications concerned with the Dessau Bauhaus buildings, their decoration & furnishing include:
Bauhaus Kolloquium Weimar 1979, Hochschule für Architektur und Bauwesen, Part 4/5, 1979 (a special publication devoted to the development of the Bauhaus and its relationship to other educational centres in Germany during the 1920s and 1930s).
Bayer, H., Gropius W. and I., *Bauhaus 1919–1928*, New York, 1938, 2nd printing Boston, 1952.
Bayer, H. et al., *50 Years Bauhaus*, catalogue of the exhibition at the Royal Academy of Arts, London, 1968.
Dearstyne, Howard, (ed. David Spaeth) *Inside the Bauhaus*, London, 1986.
Engelmann, Christine and Schädlich, Christian, *Die Bauhaus Bauten in Dessau*, Berlin, 1991.
Giedion, S., *Walter Gropius: Work and Teamwork*, London, 1954.
Gropius, Walter, *Bauhausbauten Dessau*, Bauhaus Book No. 12, Munich, 1930.
Gropius, Walter, *The New Architecture and The Bauhaus*, London, 1935 (trans. P. Morton Shand; intro by Frank Pick).
Gropius, Walter, *The Scope of Total Architecture*, London, 1956.
Isaacs, Reginald, *Walter Gropius*, Boston, 1991. (See also Professor Isaacs' article 'The Bauhaus' in **Wilkes, J.** (ed.) *Encyclopedia of Architecture: Design, Engineering and Construction*, Vol 1, New York, 1988, pp.414–21.)
Neumann, Eckhard, *Bauhaus and Bauhaus People*, New York, 1970.
Wingler, H.M., *The Bauhaus: Weimar Dessau Berlin Chicago*, Cambridge, Mass., 1969, p.627.

Bauhaus publications
Originally published as a series by Albert Langen Verlag, Munich, 1925–30. Reissued by Florian Kupferberg Verlag, Mainz, 1965–
Gropius, W., *Internationale Architektur*, 1925 (2nd edn 1927).
Klee, P. *Pädagogisches Skizzenbuch*, 1925 (2nd edn 1928). English trans. *Pedagogical Sketchbook*, London, New York, 1944.
Meyer, A. (ed.) *Ein Versuchshaus des Bauhauses in Weimar*, 1925.
Schlemmer, O., *Die Bühne im Bauhaus*, 1925. English trans: *The Theater of the Bauhaus*, Middletown, Conn., 1963.
Mondrian, P., *Neue Gestaltung*, 1925.
Van Doesburg, T., *Grundbegriffe der neuen gestaltenden Kunst*, 1925. English version *Principles of Neo-Plastic Art*, London, Greenwich, Conn., 1969.
Gropius, W. (ed.) *Neue Arbeiten der Bauhauswerkstätten*, 1925.
Moholy-Nagy, L., *Malerei, Photographie, Film*, 1925. (2nd edn *Malerei, Fotografie, Film*, 1927.) English version *Painting, Photography, Film*, London, Cambridge, Mass., 1969. (Reprinted Cambridge, Mass., 1973.)
Kandinsky, W., *Punkt und Linie zu Fläche, Beitrag zur Analyse der malerischen Elemente*, 1926 (2nd edn 1928). English trans. *Point and Line to Plane*, New York, 1947.
Oud, J.J.P., *Holländische Architektur*, 1926 (2nd edn 1929).
Malevich, K., *Die gegenstandslose Welt*, 1927. English trans. *The Non-Objective World*, Chicago, 1959.
Gropius, W., *Bauhausbauten, Dessau*, 1930.
Gleizes, A., *Kubismus*, 1928. Trilingual edn *And Cubism*, Basel, 1962.
Moholy-Nagy, L., *Von Material zu Architektur*, 1929. English trans. *The New Vision from Material to Architecture*, New York, 1930.

Photographs

Previous pages, the main elevation of the Dessau Bauhaus with its great transparent glazed workshop block.
Left, the Technical College is seen here to the left, with the workshop block beyond.
Right, the two entrances to the Technical College and the Bauhaus itself lay between the solid and transparent facades of the new building.

Previous pages, banks of opening sashes were coupled together on the workshop block facade. Above and right, the linked ranks of opening lights were controlled by a chain and pulley system that retained open windows at an equal distance.

Far left, the Bauhaus entrance. Left, the view towards the Technical College entrance.

The student *Prellerhaus* is seen here to the left with the administrative block bridge on the right.

The *Prellerhaus* balconies caused controversy among architects, because they were seen to be too decorative.

Previous pages, the celebrated sub-dividing roadway between the Technical College at the Bauhaus originally led nowhere. Today, it provides a pedestrian route through the complex. Above, the Bauhaus staircase used as part of a bent-metal chair exhibition in the building. Right, the corridor side of the administrative bridge.

The reinforced concrete structure with its shaped profile is seen here, far left, from inside a studio workshop; left, corner detail and above, the junction of the structure and curtain wall.

The administrative offices on the bridge have recently been transformed by a new colour scheme.

At the time of the 1976 refurbishment, light fittings and door furniture were renewed throughout the building.

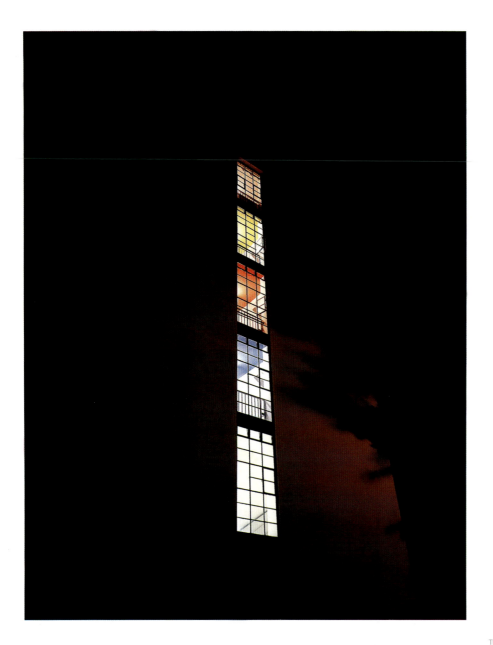

The sombre external appearance of the Bauhaus today is much enlivened by the glimpses of internal colour, seen particularly after dark.

Site plan

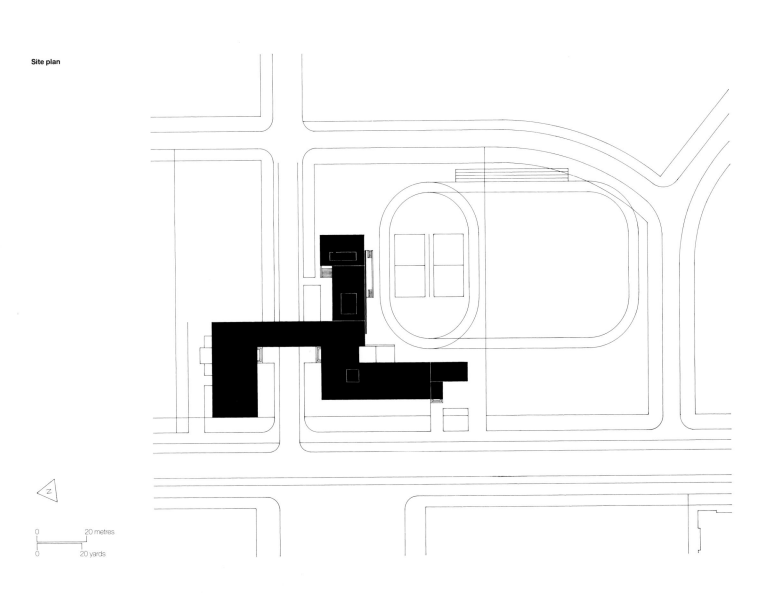

Drawings

Location plan

1. Bauhaus building
2. master's house
3. Dessau Törten Estate
4. *Konsumverein*
5. Muche's steel house
6. Fieger's house
7. balcony houses
8. labour exchange
9. Kornhaus by Fieger
10. main railway station
11. Dessau-south station
12. town hall

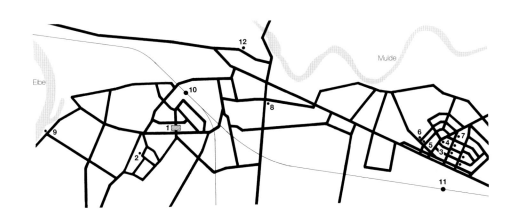

Basement plan

1. baths, gymnasium, changing rooms, laundry
2. stage workshop, printing shop, dye-works, sculpture studio, packing and stock rooms, caretaker's apartment, boiler room/coal cellar
3. laboratories, classrooms

(the exact layout is not known)

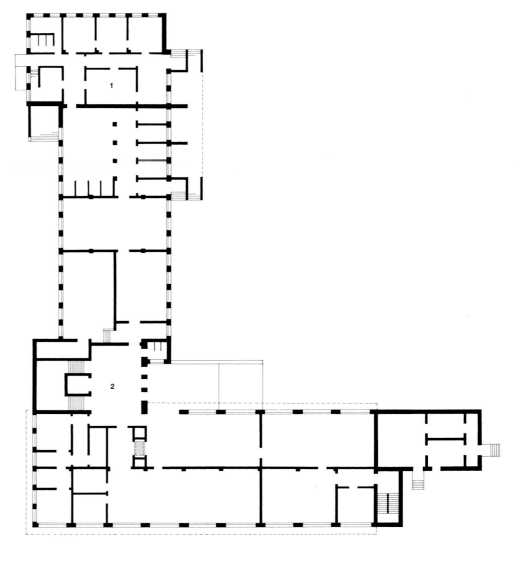

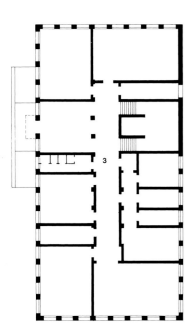

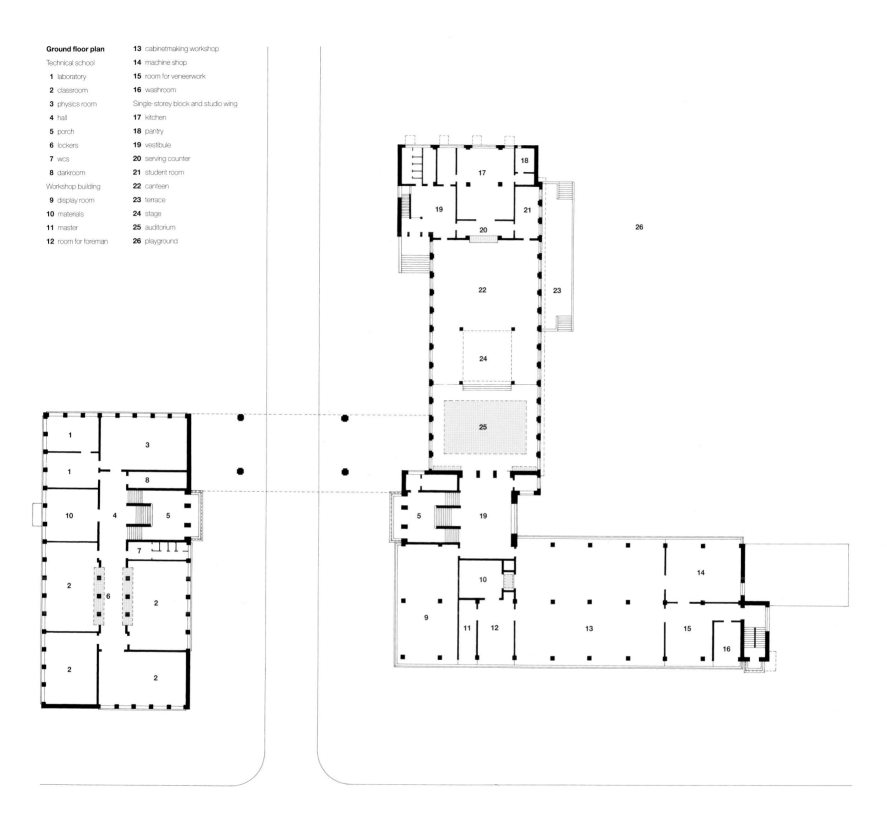

Ground floor plan
Technical school
1 laboratory
2 classroom
3 physics room
4 hall
5 porch
6 lockers
7 wcs
8 darkroom
Workshop building
9 display room
10 materials
11 master
12 room for foreman
13 cabinetmaking workshop
14 machine shop
15 room for veneerwork
16 washroom
Single-storey block and studio wing
17 kitchen
18 pantry
19 vestibule
20 serving counter
21 student room
22 canteen
23 terrace
24 stage
25 auditorium
26 playground

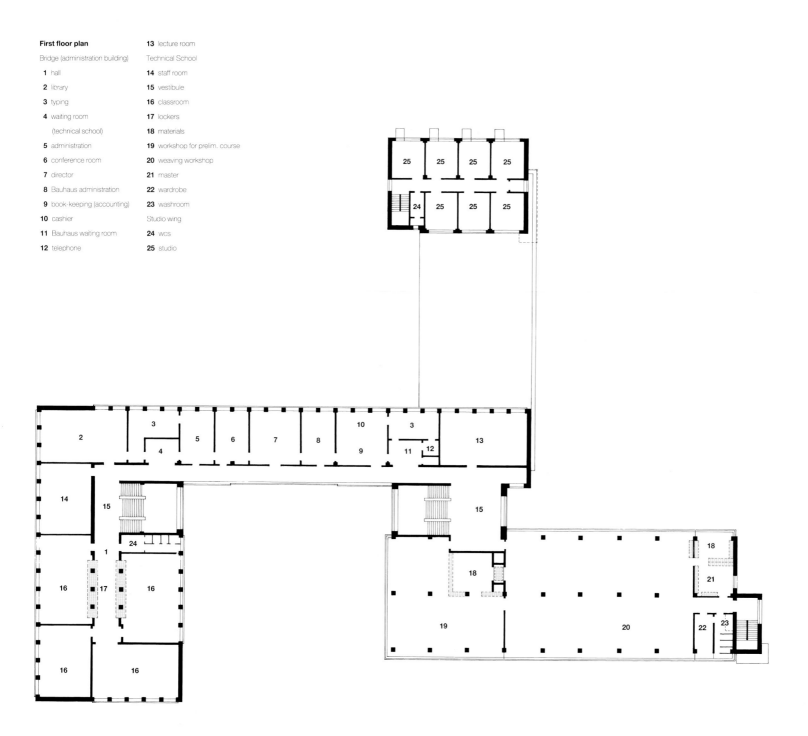

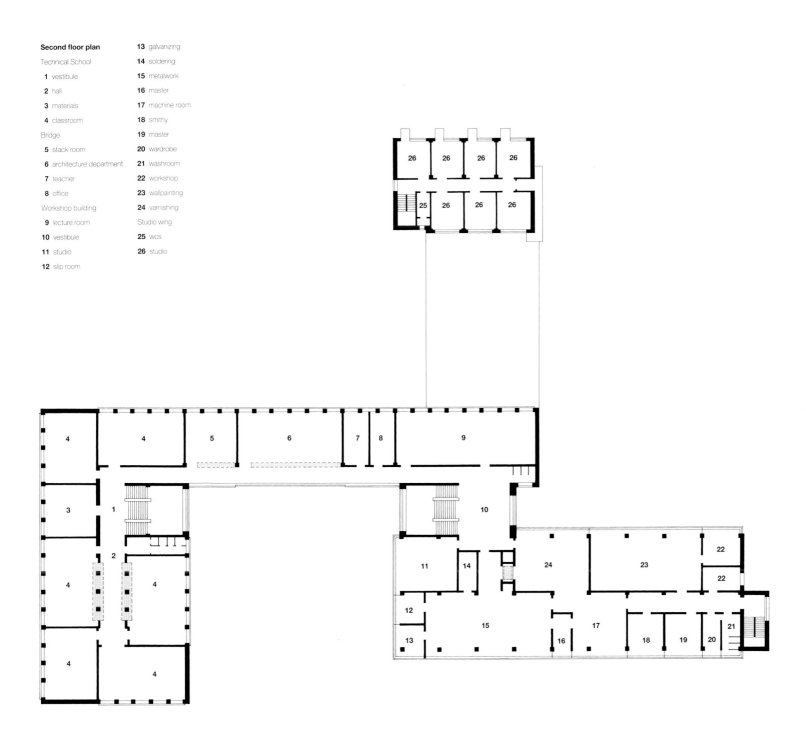

Section

through studios and workshop block

Sectional elevation

through auditorium

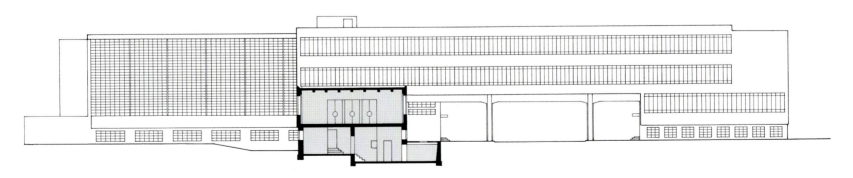

Axonometric projection

from the east

1. workshop block
2. auditorium and canteen
3. *Prellerhaus* studios
4. administration bridge
5. Technical College

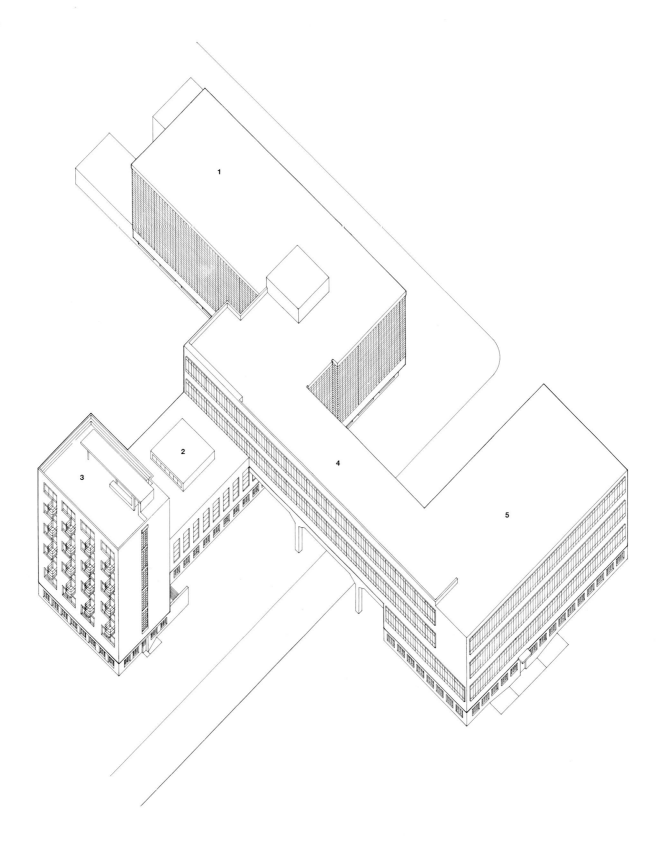

Elevation

Technical College

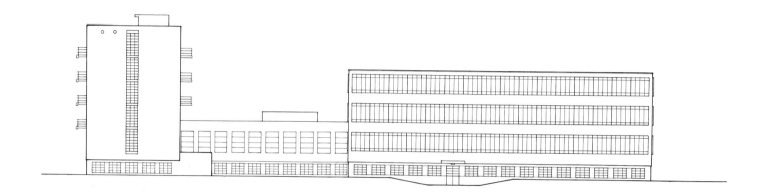

Elevation

main road of the Bauhaus

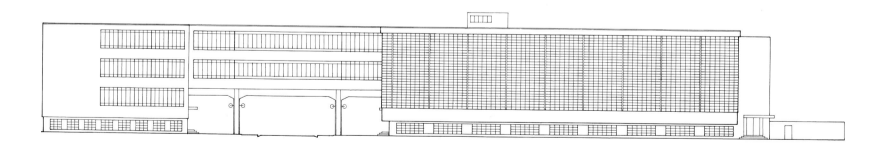

Elevation
Prellerhaus studio block

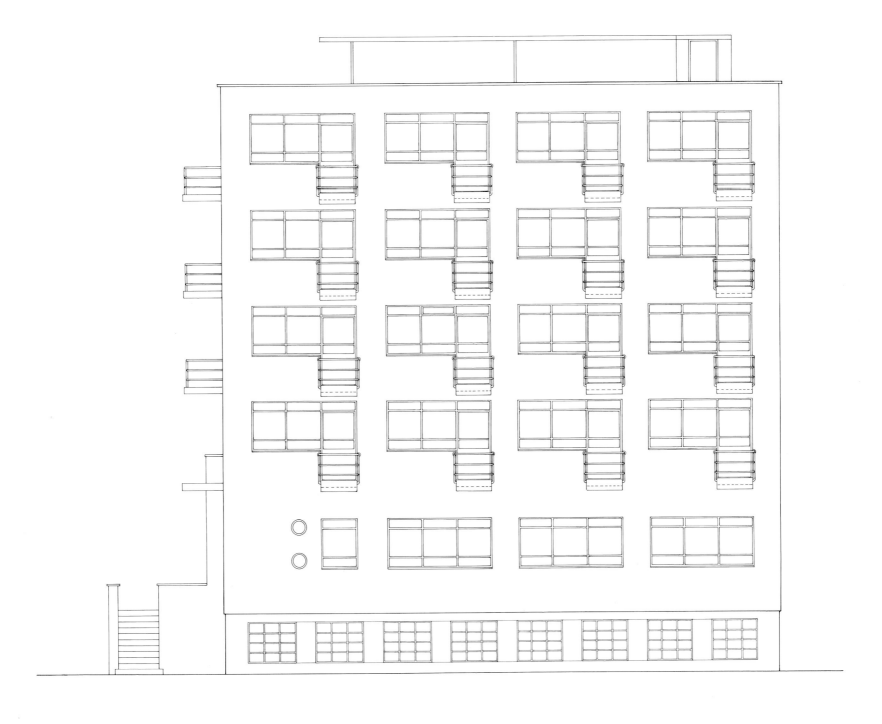

Part elevation
workshop block

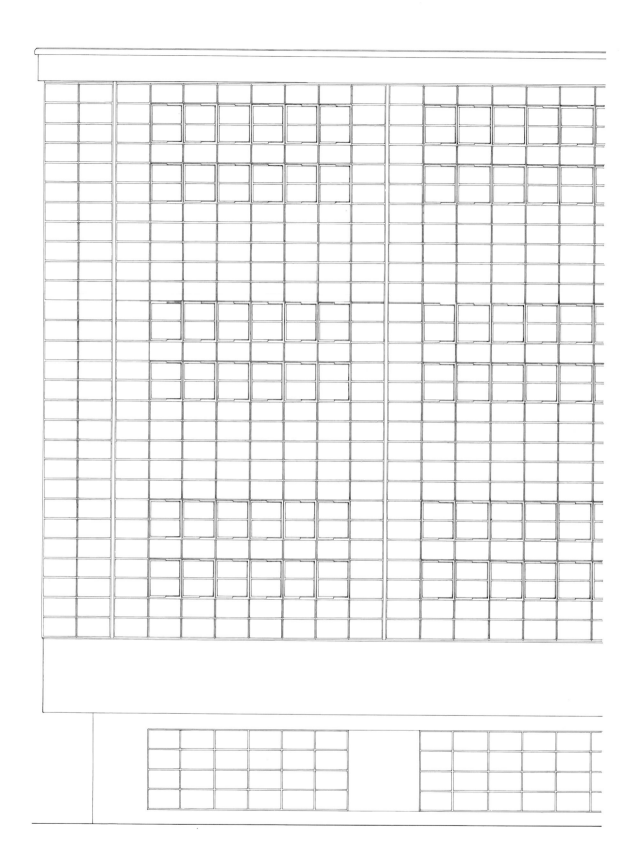

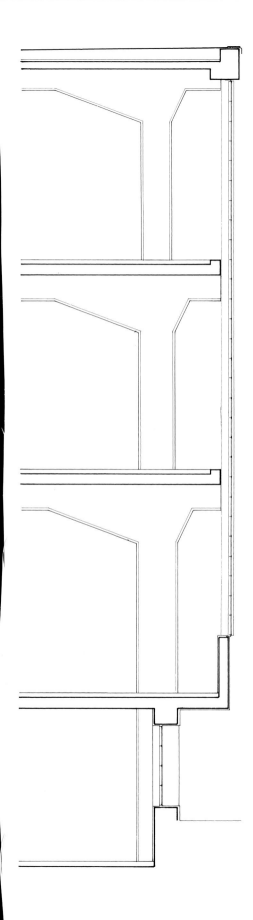

Probative section and details through perimeter of workshop block

Materials and construction as originally executed: reinforced concrete frame and floor slabs; brick infill walls; steel-framed windows, single-glazed; roofs covered with welded asphalt tiles on tortoleum-insulated base on roofs where walking was allowed, and with lacquered burlap on screed over tortoleum-insulated base where walking was not allowed.

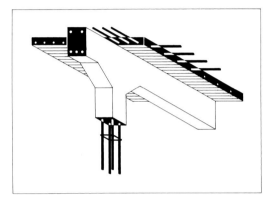

Structural detail

adapted from a contemporary source (1927)

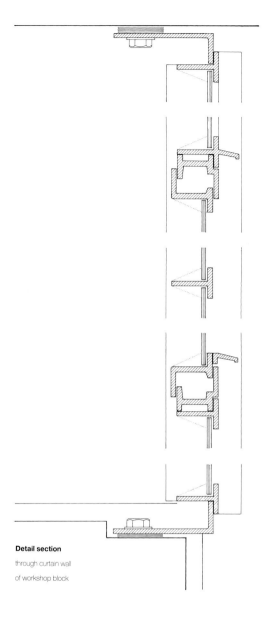

Detail section

through curtain wall of workshop block

Vertical section

through curtain wall of workshop block

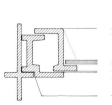
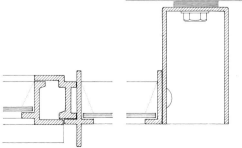

Typical plan

through curtain wall of workshop facade